Famous Explorers™

Sir Francis Drake

Tanya Larkin

The Rosen Publishing Group's
PowerKids Press™
New York

For Mr. Burke at Neshannock Elementary School,
New Castle, Pennsylvania

Published in 2001 by The Rosen Publishing Group, Inc.
29 East 21st Street, New York, NY 10010

Photo Credits: Cover and title page, pp. 2, 3, 4, 7, 8, 14, 20 © Granger Collection; p. 2, 3, 4, 9, 12 © SuperStock; p. 15 © North Wind Pictures; p.11, 16, 19 © Corbis-Bettmann; p. 2, 23 © Art Resource

First Edition

Book Design: Maria E. Melendez and Felicity Erwin

Larkin, Tanya.
   Francis Drake / by Tanya Larkin.
      p. cm.— (Famous explorers)
   Includes index.
   Summary: Describes the life and explorations of the seaman Francis Drake, the first Englishman to sail around the world.
   ISBN 0-8239-5556-7 (lib. bdg.: alk. paper)
   1. Drake, Francis, Sir, 1540?-1596—Juvenile literature. 2. Explorers—America—Biography—Juvenile literature. 3. America—Discovery and exploration—British—Juvenile literature. 4. Explorers—England—Biography—Juvenile literature. [1. Drake, Francis, Sir, 1540?-1596. 2. Explorers. 3. Admirals.] I. Title. II. Series.

E129.D7.L37 2000
942.05'5'092—dc21
[B]   99-054210

Manufactured in the United States of America

Contents

A Poor Childhood

Francis Drake was born in the 1540s in the southwestern part of England called Devon. Drake came from a poor, religious family. His father, Edmund Drake, was a **yeoman** farmer and a Protestant **preacher**. In 1549, the Drake family had to move from their home in Devon. People who believed in the Catholic religion forced those who believed in the Protestant religion to leave. The Drake family was Protestant, so they moved to the east coast of England. Their new home was on an old boat that did not work anymore. Living by the sea opened up a whole new world for young Drake.

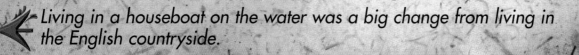
Living in a houseboat on the water was a big change from living in the English countryside.

The Life of a Young Sailor

Francis Drake learned about life at sea while he was very young. He worked as a sailor to help make money for his poor family. In 1550, when Drake was 10 years old, he was an **apprentice** on a trading ship. The ship sailed the dangerous waters of the English **Channel**. During the next few years, Drake learned how to **navigate**. He studied the position of the stars and learned how to read a compass.. He also learned how to stay away from rocks that might tear up the bottom of the ship.

Though Drake's family was poor, his cousin, John Hawkins, was rich from trading **slaves** to South and Central America. Drake wanted to work for him and get rich, too.

Drake learned to steer great sailing ships over rough waters.

Drake "The Sea Dog"

Drake went on dangerous slave-trading voyages with John Hawkins. They sold African slaves to the Spanish who lived in the Americas in return for gold and silver coins. The men's second voyage, in 1568, ended badly. The Spanish **colonists** attacked them, killing many men and harming their ships.

Drake returned to England on a small boat called the *Judith*. He wanted to get back at Spain, the richest country in the world at that time. He became a professional **pirate** or "sea dog" for the English queen, Elizabeth I. The queen gave Drake permission to sail to the Spanish **colonies** and steal their riches.

Drake's cousin John Hawkins became rich from trading slaves between Africa and the Americas. Slavery was an unjust and inhumane practice. Unfortunately, it brought wealth to some.

A View of the Pacific Ocean

In 1572, Drake and his crew of pirates set sail for Panama, a Spanish colony in Central America. There were a lot of hidden riches in Panama. Drake did not want the Spanish to find out about his plans. To this day, no one is certain of the **route** Drake took to reach the hidden riches.

When Drake reached Panama, he met some Indian slaves who had run away from their owners. Drake began to **respect** the Indian people. He promised himself that he would never trade slaves again. One of the Indians showed him a tree to climb where he could see the Caribbean Sea to the east and the Pacific Ocean to the west. Until then, only the Spanish had sailed on the Pacific Ocean. Drake knew he would sail on the Pacific one day.

Drake came to respect the Indians (above). Drake stole gold and silver from the Spanish (below).

Spain

Drake's Welcome Home

With the help of the Indians, Drake stole a large amount of silver from the Spanish. He returned to Plymouth, England, in 1573 with these riches. The townspeople welcomed home their hero. Drake was rich and famous, but Queen Elizabeth I was upset. England was trying to make peace with Spain. Even though the queen had given Drake permission to be a pirate and steal from the Spanish, she was worried that Drake's actions might start a war with Spain.

Spain and England did not get along well because Spain's king was Catholic and England's queen was Protestant. The queen did not mind some **conflict** with Spain, but she did not want to start a war. It was decided that Drake should leave England until things calmed down.

Queen Elizabeth I worried that Drake's actions would cause a war with Spain.

Secret Orders From the Queen

In 1577, Queen Elizabeth I gave Drake money to sail around South America to the Pacific Ocean. She told Drake to make trading agreements with South American Indians. She also secretly ordered Drake to surprise the Spanish and **loot** their riches. Her order was a secret because she did not want King Philip of Spain to know that she supported Drake.

In addition to trading and looting, Drake was told to try to find the western end of a **waterway** that connected the Atlantic and Pacific Oceans. This waterway was called the Northwest Passage.

A portrait of King Philip of Spain (above). Spain had many powerful ships (right).

Panic on the High Seas

On November 15, 1577, Drake left Plymouth harbor in England, with five ships. Drake did not tell anyone where he was going. This way the Spanish would not find out his plans. When the crew reached the African coast, Drake announced that he really hoped to reach the Pacific Ocean.

The crew panicked. They believed that fires near the **equator** would burn them to ashes and huge water snakes would squeeze the ships into pieces. Most of all, they feared the **Straits** of Magellan at the tip of South America. Many people had died in ships that had crashed into rocks there. Thomas Doughty, one of the sailors, questioned Drake's plan. When Drake found out, he accused Doughty of being a **traitor**. To teach his crew a lesson, Drake ordered that Doughty be killed.

Drake's ships let down their sails when they reached the shore.

Adventures in the Pacific

It took Drake 16 days to pass the Straits of Magellan. Strong winds blew against the ships, and mountains **towered** on either side. Sailors from the country of Wales saw birds that could not fly. They called the birds pen gwyns, which means "white heads" in Welsh. That is how penguins got their name.

On an island off the coast of Chile, Indians welcomed Drake's **fleet** to land. Drake traded cloth and colored beads for chickens, vegetables, and sheep. The next day, Drake and 12 men rowed to shore. As they tied up their boat, the Indians made a surprise attack. Drake's crew barely escaped. Drake and his sailors left the Indians and attacked Spanish towns and ships. They loaded their ships with so much Spanish gold that the ships almost sunk.

Sometimes the Indians and the explorers traded with each other. Other times they fought.

Around the World

Drake had to figure out how to get home with the precious **booty**. His crew did not want to sail the Straits of Magellan again. The Spanish would be there. Drake stopped in what is now California and claimed it for the queen. He sailed north to what is now Vancouver, Canada, but still could not find the Northwest Passage. Finally he decided that the best way to get home was by sailing west. He sailed west all the way around the world. He reached the Spice Islands on November 4, 1579. These were the islands that Christopher Columbus had set out to find when he accidentally landed on the shores of the Americas.

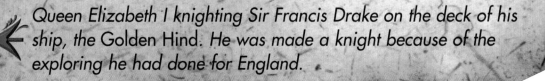

Queen Elizabeth I knighting Sir Francis Drake on the deck of his ship, the Golden Hind. He was made a knight because of the exploring he had done for England.

A Pirate Becomes a Knight

In September 1580, Drake returned to Plymouth, England. He became the first person to sail around the world and live to tell about it. Still, his life was in danger. King Philip of Spain demanded that Queen Elizabeth I kill Drake. Queen Elizabeth I went aboard Drake's ship. Drake knelt before her. She smiled and said, "The king of Spain has asked for your head. Now I will have it." She touched his shoulder with a sword and made him a **knight**.

Sir Francis Drake Timeline

1540–Born in Devon, England.

1573–Drake returns to England with stolen Spanish treasure.

1577–Drake sets off to search for the Northwest Passage.

1580–Drake returns to England after sailing around the world.

Glossary

apprentice (uh-PREN-tis) A young person learning a trade.

booty (BOO-tee) Riches taken during a war or battle.

channel (CHA-nul) A body of water that joins two larger bodies of water.

colonies (KAH-luh-nees) Areas in new countries where large groups of people move, who are still ruled by the leaders and laws of their old countries.

colonists (KAH-luh-nists) People who live in a colony.

conflict (KON-flikt) A fight or a struggle.

equator (ih-KWAY-tur) An imaginary line around Earth that separates it into two parts, north and south.

fleet (FLEET) A group of ships.

knight (NYT) A man given a high rank in the military because of his service to the king or queen.

loot (LOOT) To steal.

navigate (NA-vuh-gayt) To explore the sea.

pirate (PY-rit) A person who attacks and robs ships.

preacher (PREE-chur) A person whose job it is to give talks about religion.

respect (ree-SPEKT) To think highly of someone or something.

route (ROOT) The path you take to get somewhere.

slaves (SLAYVS) People who are "owned" by others and forced to work for them.

straits (STRAYTS) Passageways between two bodies of water.

towered (TAU-werd) To stand very high above something.

traitor (TRAY-tur) A person who turns against his or her country.

waterway (WAH-ter-way) A river, canal, or other body of water that ships use.

yeoman (YO-men) A person who owns and takes care of a small farm.

Index

Web Sites:

To learn more about Sir Francis Drake, check out these Web sites:

http://www.optonline.com/comptons/ceo/01387_A.html

http://legends.dm.net/pirates/drake.html

http://www.win.tue.nl/cs/fm/engels/discovery